T0167684

TRUTHS OF THE UNREMEMBERED THINGS

PAUL WILKINS

Truths of the
Unremembered Things

CARCANET

First published in 1999 by
Carcanet Press Limited
4th Floor, Conavon Court
12-16 Blackfriars Street
Manchester M3 5BQ

A CIP catalogue record for this book
is available from the British Library
ISBN 1 85754 402 1

The publisher acknowledges financial assistance
from the Arts Council of England

Set in 10pt Plantin by Bryan Williamson, Frome
Printed and bound in England by SRP Ltd, Exeter

Contents

Acknowledgements

A number of these poems, some in different form, first appeared in the magazines *PN Review* and *The Honest Ulsterman,* and in the anthology *Gay Love Poetry* (Robinson, 1997). 'Effects' was first published in *Gay Love Poetry* under the pseudonym Richard Essenden.

At the Fort, Grianan

for Sean McMahon

End of a summer, and the cars
Change gear, head inland.
We turn off to the hilltop, and look back.

The view of the old kingdom:
Down there, from beach to homes
The motions tinily continue,

Soundless, soon lost in the sense of
Miles, height, air,
Wide light steering over the bronze waters.

On the ramparts, restored
With nothing to defend,
I point the camera to avoid

The litter-bin, the boy in a red jersey,
Two women gazing upwards
As if dazed. But the picture cannot hold

Something not in the stone, the wind, the warmth;
In only ourselves, our words,
My sickness to be single in such a place

That could resist nothing,
Shadow trapped inside.
So few words I have for this wall of rubble

And still too many.
One can hardly love this world,
Wanting it empty.

We stoop through a passage to the dusk
And all our lives, the light there
Narrowing, sharper.

Glasnost'

The month Ivan's and Misha's tank whined
juddering into Wenceslas Square,
I passed O-level Russian.

'Fascinating,' grins Alastair,
who is listening to these lines.

August 1968: 'Socialism's human face' was
Dubcek's, a poster on a Clapham bedroom wall, his thin mouth
smiling under tired, vulture eyes. In Croydon we heard
Prague Radio crackling, deciphered the chalked tank-turrets'
'Volodya, go home! Your Anna is with Fyodor!'

I still have some of the Russian words.
Kak vas zavoot? I can ask someone.
'What do they call you?' 'What is your name?'
Chai s'limonom, parzhalsta. I can order a cup of lemon tea.
I know that *Glasnost'* must be a noun.

And I remember Lenin's question: What is to be done?
The man who taught us how to ask *Shto delat'?* was
'obviously queer'. That August
he tried to persuade me I should take the subject further.
I went for Economics, collaborated in the rumours.

Throughout that year, Chris had sat two desks ahead of me.
First in our class to wear flared trousers,
he knew irregular Greek verbs and the Russian for
'I understand the lesson for today.'
I didn't and I don't.

I know that at the end of *Glasnost'* is a sound
my language can't write down.
The 'soft sign', they call it. It's a little
'tch' of tenderness, a gentle chafing of the teeth and tongue.
No, that's not it.

'But you can say it, can't you? And who was Chris?' Alastair
pours us beers. 'And Lenin – for Christ's sake, Lenin!'

Decades on, two pairs of flares hang
embarrassed in my wardrobe. I open the window
on an August night in London, and the raining random noise
spits in and on:

traffic; the pulse of music from the Seventh Day Adventist Hall;
a dog two streets away,
barking with furious thirst or boredom,
chafing at the chain of speech he does not have.

In the paper Boris Zhikov, aged 16,
clutches his signed LP above a headline:
Children of Perestroika Meet the Pet Shop Boys.

I close and lock the window.
I watch my video of Horovitz
playing at last again in Moscow after sixty years.
Rachmaninov, Scriabin, Schumann's *Kinderszenen.*
During the 'Träumerei' encore, a tear slides down an old man's cheek.

'The trouble with your poems is,' says Alastair,
'you don't say enough about your feelings.'

I rehearse the phrases that have stayed:
Kak menya zavoot? and *Shto delat'?*
What do they call me? What is to be done?
A sound of tenderness, is it?
The teeth against the tongue.

'But you can say it, can't you?' Alastair repeats.
He finishes his beer and grins again.
'And by the way, that isn't how you spell my name.'

The dictionary I found this summer translates
Glasnost' as, not 'openness', but 'publicity'.

At its end is something I can't yet write down.

9

The Drum-Bridge at Kameido

Two men are crossing the drum-bridge at Kameido,
laughing and talking together.
They do this in a print by Hokusai.
Below them runs the torrent of the river.

It seems to be near to dusk.
When they climb the steep curve of the bridge
their high wooden shoes
clack on the cross-slats, they almost

totter, as if trying to walk a tight-rope.
They sway to the crest of the bridge,
then pause, rest their elbows on the parapet
and face down to the waters.

From a house on the far side
faint notes of the shamisen and koto
gather and drift and dissolve,
the waters rushing below.

The men have drunk themselves into
that first numb haze.
It will pass, as they stand
leaning on the parapet and looking down

vacantly at the river, the breeze
cooling their shaven foreheads.
They laugh together and reminisce
(they have shared so many lovers);

they delight to hear of each's conquest
of those the other wanted. And of those bought,
why would any not be glad to know
their youth could be worth buying?

So it is, in the hidden empires of hunger and requital.
Inside the houses these two men will enter soon,
their lovers of tonight, perfuming their olive skin,
combing the oiled black locks on their foreheads,

are waiting in the mist behind frail paper walls.
So it is, in the provinces of patience,
along the shaded rivers of what seems relief.
The shamisen twangs one more exquisite dissonance.

The lovers' long-sleeved kimonos will fall open
soon, hands will caress hairless chests,
the men will lie down naked with their lovers,
breathing. Ten yards from here,

at the end of the drum-bridge, these two will
bow slightly and part. For now, for ten yards,
they reminisce and laugh.
Little of all this is depicted in the print by Hokusai

of the drum-bridge at Kameido,
sometime in the 1820s.
Below the bridge,
cold waters boil and surge away.

America

Imagining America, I am driving the car
(I can't drive) westwards from Ohio
across prairies of shaking wheat,
through the Dakotas, on from Idaho into Oregon.

The car is a Dodge or a Studebaker – no, a vintage
Duesenberg. Its chrome glints in Wichita or Albuquerque,
as I stare out from my motel window
at blue midnight snowfields.

Late in April, I stop somewhere on the plains
to call a man in Memphis collect.
A waitress with a chipped tooth
serves me eggs and coffee in a diner.

Her name is Jackie; her husband is at home,
in jeans, checked shirt and rimless spectacles,
painting the outhouse a piercing white;
he is thinking of how they will save their lives.

And I go far on, my feet flexed
against the rubbered pedals, staring ahead
along the straight roads of Montana,
down the highways through Wyoming into Nebraska.

The height and perfect blue of a Kansas sky.
Cindered steelworks and clanking crossings,
the sad and glowing vastnesses.
In Minnesota and New Mexico

what innocence and what exhaustion,
what reticence in Oshkosh, Wisconsin,
in Intercourse, Pennsylvania,
in Recluse, Wyoming.

The lives there in America, where one supreme obscenity is *mother*,
where the stilled towns try to talk to God.
Patriotism, farms and foreclosures, pornography,
silos of grain and warheads, the porch-lights coming on.

In Flagstaff, Arizona. In Leadville, in Media,
in Spearfish, Massacre Rocks, Cascade.
What is it that so many are remembering in the dark
in Topeka, in Aladdin and in Fredericksburg?

I think of the pilots of boats
on the west branch of the Susquehanna River,
finding their course northwards to Athens,
circling and dropping their plumb-lines like lassoes . . .

They stand upright again, shielding their eyes
against that brilliance above the peaks,
languidly saluting. And I
am imagining America,

longing for those distances.
I need more gas and cigarettes,
I need to know how far the turning for Columbus is.
I need to know those lives of men and women

in Normal and in Warsaw, Illinois.
They are waiting for their husbands,
for their lovers and betrayers, soon arriving
in hushed America on the late-afternoon trains.

Agoraphobia

Afterwards I'll speak a memory of words, and it will say:
They run from me; they used to hunt me down.

This night, and anonymous us in the cage of our escapes.
Heat of us in the secret room. We're loving, bewildered,
Each asking who's who: hunter, hunted. Each demanding.

Forgotten, any answer. Cold fuzzes the panes of water we step
    homewards on.
Over pale skin, the faltering hands spread, squandering these
    seconds.
Reality was when we were fifteen, and everything was
Under the hammer. Bid for, beaten flat, our lusts sleep
Mad and stumbling with poor dreams, try to wake, want to,
    gesture it, don't.

Walking from Fairlight

Trembling sea,
as if some vast shock has touched it;
but nothing has,

and least the mind
hushed with static of the surf
homing to its station.

To have walked this far,
at dusk, along the Firehills,
might prove a symmetry in the world,

how it signals human patterns;
the gnarled moon at dusk
beginning to throw down

its faintest silver stairway.
Wherever you stand,
it reaches to you.

The brooks run through furze
into haze. A couple stroll
this way along the firebreak,

and I turn back, asking,
staring across a field of stubble,
hearing all answers

hush through shingle.
Distant, lulling, alien speech,
sibilant peace; trembling sea,

as if some love had touched me.
Moon throws down its silver stairway.
Wherever I stand,

it reaches to me.
A thirst
slavers over Mercator's oceans.

The Avenue, Middleharnis

They make you giddy with their height,
the almost branchless trees
flanking the avenue at Middleharnis.

This canvas was painted sometime in the seventeenth century,
probably as an exercise in perspective.
The artist was Hobbema, who lived to be 75 or 76.

Down the dirt-track avenue towards us
a man strides with his dog.
On this postcard I am peering at, the man is

so far away, that maybe it's not a dog,
trotting beside him and lifting its head towards its master,
seeking that look of affirmation;

perhaps instead the man in his broad-brimmed hat and gaiters
pushes some kind of barrow,
loaded with dung or produce,

down the road that widens like a wake from him to us.
But it is we who are sailing on,
it is he who is drowning in the enormous years.

Still, along the avenue at Middleharnis,
accompanied by his pet or burden,
the man seems to walk as if alive.

Consider what extents of time since then.
Consider the clearances, the building,
the tracks of armies, the slamming of car-doors.

In the painting there are flimsy clouds in the sky,
a distant church-tower to the left.
Nearer, on the right, some kind of barn,

and two people stood beside it talking.
Along the avenue at Middleharnis
the slender, almost branchless trees

make you giddy with their height.
How they must have swayed in the wind there
but in your eye they are frozen.

Centuries, distances,
incomprehensibles. People see
the world, they act this way.

Flights

Again in the afternoon, that ridiculous
beauty – a cauliflower landscape as we rise
into a sunspill flickering.

White, shuddering silence,
the numbers running down to zero,
a film too far back for words.

Strapped in, I watch
blank frames of my noisy life begin.
Or, by night, I scan

linked lights of the motorways below:
a dizziness of galaxies, or blur of molecules,
busy with chains of purpose.

Behind me, tomorrow, a skater
cuts patterns on a pond,
shapes invisible from this height,

his face held smiling
up to the stupid, imperative light,
his arms clasped behind him, as if bound.

Plots

There are things which do not fit
Any plan; and what is called life
Looses such hailing, random arrows,
And not for love,
Or pain even –

But you must be hero in the myth of your life,
Wry Gulliver picking stray barbs from his neck.
And the glass man on the wall repeats,
Repeats. And you must again inherit
Your stopped heart, the broken clock,

Sipping at what you have done,
Have always done, in this same bed lie
Down in this plot again with these
Stone words above you saying
When ended, when began.

The god who charmed you
Tugs sheets around his head,
As if to sleep.
We speak the names we have.
Alone with pronouns, we insist on fate.

January 8th

In the early hours, another heavy fall:
Dry snow, they say it could lie for days.
You have gone south.

Mind rhymes with its world.

So many degrees below:
In such cold, each hugs himself,
Each mimes his love alone.

Hush of a drummer's brush across the skin.

The New Year,
The feast of Epiphany,
The coldest night in two decades.

When will you bring yourself home through the snow?

Hunched at the window, I see
Fields and roads lose boundaries,
I try to read some wide, white synonym . . .

I tell myself, there are such metaphors to be made from this.

But soon I am out walking, noticing
These flakes that bind to shroud the world
Vanishing on bared wrists, in the open palm.

And does that mean anything?

And 3D are back now from their break,
Grinning, their hair clotted with white.
We open our poetry books; today, dramatic monologues.

And the news announces blizzards in the south.

Hall of Mirrors

At Notre Dame, the great rose-window:
A child's immense kaleidoscope,
A pattern of fragments and each moment's sunlight
Held for centuries. We robed, and sang.

The previous night at Charenton,
I intoned the 'Ave Verum'
Drunk beneath a mattress;
Shy Jim Keating cursed and hit out at the monks.

Easter 1970: our school choir loose in Paris
With cheap wine, hunchback jokes and souvenirs;
Chris talking in the dusk . . . Still memory
Holds those moments for some reason, keeps shaking

Their splintered pointless secret.
Years further down that tunnel,
So much more jagged coloured glass
Heaps up against the light.

At Versailles we filed past the grubby gilt.
A master told us how nobility
Pissed in the narrow corridors.
The history tour: disillusion's glamour.

And in the Hall of Mirrors, named
Like a fairground giggle, no skinny giants
Or dwarves rippling with fat.
Just the flat, stained mirrors,

And in them our pale, half-children's faces.
And stretching before us in the place of broken treaty,
A pattern of gardens empty in the rain,
Blossoming with fountains, glassy green.

The Donkey, the Buttocks

Lost of course somehow,
that photograph where they are standing early in the Thirties
behind the house in Bermondsey,
a father and his two sons, all in waistcoats,
the chains of pocket-watches drooping at their fronts.

Three decades later my guardian uncle,
almost wealthy, gave me this advice:
Kindly move into the garden if you have to break wind.
He favoured a long patrician vowel when he called
anyone a fool: silly ass, he meant.

Arse, it sounded like.
How did he get that voice?
Saying to his wife: *The boy's neck and blazer are quite filthy.*
Saying in hotels and shops: *The boy will take the beef.*
We wish to purchase a suit for the boy.

One more strangeness on a lengthy roll:
two cars, a nightly bath, the tennis-lessons, holidays in hotels,
the leaded lozenges on all the windows.
And when I inched open the heavy drawer in the bedroom,
the sketchbooks of Michelangelo.

Uncle drew the outside of his mock Tudor house
and used it for the cover of his Christmas cards.
The night before I left for boarding-school he sketched
a version of the facts of life, explained his childless marriage,
inscribed the inside of my trunk in faultless upper case

with my name, his address.
The first half-term, I had to be *chastised* for lying.
He came into the bathroom, turned the radio up loud,
made me take off all my clothes.
Thirty years more and he was dead.

I dressed in the bathroom and brushed my language,
the radio still up loud to drown a wordless noise of mine.
On my answering-machine, a voice apologised
for being absent, a voice that's still not
quite what's wanted promised to reply.

I trudged up Putney Hill through deep snow
to his funeral by the Common;
I joined in with the same hymns I'd have chosen for my own.
Outside I lit a *Senior Service*, my father's brand,
returning extinguished matches backwards in the box.

Thursday

You can't say what it is.
A Thursday music, with no libretto.

That last afternoon you can remember with your mother:
the lawn half trodden away, the vast damp sheets
thrapping on the line; a grey sky beyond,
and the windows she had polished
so clean onto forever.

Is it only in words that we find our lives?
You were too young, so they failed you.
Now they are the everything that smokes a shape on nothing.

What you look back to,
always too hazed to be understood or forgiven.
A tall sky there beyond you.
What you look onward to, its nameless melting.

Secrets no one hid or knew to keep.
Each in its lost years, certain, waiting for you.

The Will

The will is a corridor,
a corridor of unmarked rooms.

Behind the door you choose
an old man sits at a desk,

dictating. He says this is
his will, to be here,

naming himself, you,
the various gifts,

plotting what it is brings
you to this room and him.

Is he behind whichever door you choose
or must you choose this one?

Too late when, looking up,
he has the face that will be yours,

hands that are yours waving
furiously back the wrong visitor,

pointing to the corner where
a boy sits drowsing, taking down

words inexactly,
almost dreaming of some corridor,

the doors all standing open,
and someone entering and finding no one
or a figure rising from his chair to be you.

Effects

1

This is the poem I have to write.
This is the poem I have to write to you.

2

Years back, you made me a copy of your will.
Now I do whatever you require.

Your coffin slides to the furnace;
on the tape your living fingers

stroke out the notes of
I'd like to get you

on a slow boat to China,
all by myself alone

and then I wince and almost want to giggle
as the tune shifts into

All of me, why not take all of me . . .
I take the cheque,

await delivery of the TV, stereo, freezer.
And I drink the whisky left in your house

quickly, its raw warmth seeming my throat's
right, blighted inheritance.

3

The name you chose when they made you a monk.
The name of wisdom.

What happened in your childhood, and went
echoing on in mine? And later.

Back to the first cause
we can't go

but there is a sentence, commanding the child to be severed in two
and one part to be given to each of those claiming him.

4
Start of a spell of nearly perfect weather more than thirty years ago.
You walked into the quadrangle and paused,
hearing notes trickling from an open window, recognised
with a sweet shock the piano you had given up,
its tone to you as unmistakeable as your mother's voice.

How many times did you tell me that?
Once you'd left, she couldn't bear to keep the keys you'd played.
A mother's love, turned to a fragrance like retribution.
She gave the piano to the old school; a year beyond her death,
you went to work there. Too neat, the way things happened to you.

And so it was you walked into the sun-flooded quad,
and heard that monk in his eighties trying
clumsy arpeggios in an exercise of childhood.
Months later he died in your arms
and you woke up the dormitory at one a.m. to make us pray.

What happened to those cracked, nicotined ivories?
Twenty years after, in your cramped spare bedroom
there was a brand new baby grand you never played.
It's all like irony, but harsher.
I've given your records away.

But still I can see the fingers that had touched me
caressing some keyboard, practising your favourites:
Chopin, Brahms, Rachmaninov. You taught me to love

the ones you loved but now in my long defeat
I cherish listening to the Britten you hated
(nice touch, you watched the opera of *Death in Venice* with the
    sound off).

And in my proper life I hear clean solitary notes of Satie,
falling as if like droplets from raised oars
in a boat my unborn brother is rowing on the almost silent distance
    of a lake.

5
Orphaned and at boarding-school,
happier away from my childless guardian's 'home',

I soon knew those corrupted kindnesses of yours,
soon depended on them.

You see, I write 'corrupted'.
Every time I try to want to write of your kindness,

I think of more to condemn.
Of course I write this only now you're dead.

6
At 13, 14, I thought I knew
I wanted to live a grown man's life.

But those Saturdays went on and on:
as the wrestling began on TV, your office-door's Yale-snib clicking

locked; the red light going on; then always
the slither of your palm across the backs of my bared thighs.

The heady sweetness of that green liqueur you gave me.
Embarrassments; mysteries. And arousals.

And those corrupted kindnesses of yours that I relied on.
Afterwards the sneers and jealousies of Larry Pearson, David Hewitt,

John and Peter Cowan, Alex Lord.
Even their fictitious names strike home.

I didn't know for years the permutations they went through
in each others' beds; or with you, in two or three locked rooms:

Larry and John at Larry's house one weekend;
David in shorts for you, drunk and eager, waiting hidden behind
    the desk;

Peter and Alex in the dorm after you'd been gone a week;
and, later, when Alex met you at the country-hotel, you posing as
    his uncle . . .

Who was it who set off the ticking metronomes of these lives?
All of them (at 13, 14) going in with you

and hearing the click of the Yale-lock on your office-door,
all of them sent into the small back-room to change . . .

To change, but to be the same forever.
That age. That look. That innocence,

but aroused, responsive. That lost thing never lost.
What of all this should be forgiven?

All of it, perhaps. None of it's ever forgotten.
I have to imagine John Cowan nearly naked close to midnight in
    your bedroom,

the rest of us sleeping in the dorm just yards away.
He knelt (you said), his elbows on your bed, like a prayer come true.

As he awaited you, his penis stiffening (I guess from what you said),
what was John thinking then? And does he wait and want to think
    of it again

now, thirty years on, even when with a woman or a wife perhaps?
You used to say that, in our marriages and affairs,

you'd have us always in your grip. Alex and John,
who won't read this, I wish they could tell me if it's true

desire's an unposted road, offering no other route to the island.
I wish they could speak to me the different shapes of what they've
    lived

with men or women. Where I am,
memory is sleepless, must keep on going through it all again.

The red light coming on.

The green liqueur.

The small room at the back.

The thin white cotton shorts.

Click of the lock.

7
Each night, I hear the radio's Shipping Bulletin
speak the name of where you lived.

A small, dull town.
I think of the grey sea quivering, rushing for miles

towards the pleasure-arcades, towards the white-walled
three-quarters-empty hotels.

We hardly ever tried to speak of consequences,
the distinct and random cause.

And now you've gone utterly beyond my words
as I lie listening to the radio intone its forecast,

its warning, its entrancement:
Haze. Calm. Four miles. Rising slowly.

8

When you pulled those nervous, pliant boys of 13, 14, 15
face-down across your lap,
their buttocks taut inside thin brief shorts,
what was it you were hoping for?

And the ones aged 17, 18, 19,
who needed no commanding to comply,
why did they seek with you their versions of pleasure, of contempt?
You'd lament they couldn't still be 13, 14, 15.

Alex, John, the others –
locked into your dream, inside an airless childhood,
they gasped at their lives,
flinching their clenched willingness against your falling hand.

9

After lights-out, the locker was opened
and I glimpsed the brunette with big breasts
lifting her soft cleavage to me, leering.

That was 1965,
the autumn I discovered masturbation,
dreaming of the fly-half of the second XV.

I shared a room with Jerzy,
the blond half-Polish boy
who wore the briefest gym-shorts in the school.

PRIVACY

Also by Justin Quinn from Carcanet

The 'O'o'a'a' Bird

PRIVACY

JUSTIN QUINN

CARCANET

First published in 1999 by
Carcanet Press Limited
4th Floor, Conavon Court
12–16 Blackfriars Street
Manchester M3 5BQ

A CIP catalogue record for this book
is available from the British Library.
ISBN 1 85754 416 1

The publisher acknowledges financial assistance
from the Arts Council of England.

Set in Bembo by XL Publishing Services, Tiverton
Printed and bound in Great Britain by SRP Ltd, Exeter

FOR DAVID WHEATLEY

ACKNOWLEDGEMENTS

I would like to thank the following for their help and comments over the last few years: Brendan F. Dempsey, Robert Cremins, Selina Guinness, Aisling Maguire, Sinéad Morrissey, Michael Schmidt, and lastly, David Wheatley, to whom this book is dedicated.

Thanks are also due to the editors of the following publications in which some of the poems first appeared: *College Green*, *HU*, *The Irish Review*, *The Irish Times*, *Oxford Poetry*, *Poetry Ireland Review*, *PN Review*, *Poetry Review*, *Thumbscrew*, *Quadrant*, *Verse*. 'Insomnia' was published as a broadsheet in a limited edition of 250 copies by Bernard Stone at Turret Books (London, March 1997).

Grateful acknowledgement is made to Liveright Publishing Corporation for permission to reprint part of Hart Crane's *The Bridge*, and to Academia Publishers for the passage from Jan Patočka's *Kacířské eseje o filosofii dějin* (Prague, 1990).

CONTENTS

So, must we from the hawk's far stemming view,
Must we descend as worm's eye to construe
Our love of all we touch . . .

— HART CRANE, *The Bridge*

Na nejdůležitější modifikaci, kterou přinesly pozdější představy, upozornila H. Arendtová, když poukázala k tomu, že sféra domu nyní není jádrem světa vůbec, že je to pouze soukromá sféra, vedle níž vystoupila v Řecku a Římì jiná neméně důležitá a jí oponující sféra veřejnosti.

— JAN PATOČKA, *Kacířské eseje o filosofii dějin*

LANDSCAPE BY BUS

Look out the window – half
A landscape, half its trees.
Switch focus. Reflections of
The rest float by on these.

At sixty miles an hour
The world's being folded back
Into a suitcase. Where
Oh where will I unpack?

6.55 A. M.

5
Abseiling down
A rope that stretches from an Alpine height
For miles through rising temperatures to the small town
Tucked neatly in one corner of the valley floor
At such a speed, I have about
Five seconds left before
I brace and light;

4
While you're banking
With two advisers and the Premier
Above the city in the government jet, outflanking
Them with four minutes to go before you land
And they stride out to face the press
And make, as you have planned,
The country tremor;

3
While I'm going faster
Down a graph-curve about the anti-beef craze
And its effects on GNP (a clear disaster) . . .
Time equals T and three more units to the Crash
You were at pains to show the Premier –
One of the sheets you stash
Back in your briefcase;

2
And as events
Go swirling wildly out of order, you
Drive from the airport in your dusk-pink Italian Ventos
(Roadholding good on corniche and in wet conditions)
For two hours to the valley town
I'll land in in two seconds
Just as you come to

1
A braking halt,
With still time on the way to engineer
A last minute affair that is nobody's fault.
Now everything's happening so fast, the way we glance
And swerve by mountains, phalloi, parents,
The intervening distance
Approaching zer-

0.
Stopped dead,
Come skidding out of pastiche, out of text,
Into another that has us side by side in bed
With seven bells, we bathe here in a giga-watt
Of sunlight, dazed and twined together
And not sure as to what
Will happen next.

A STRAND OF HAIR

I never asked you for your hand,
Or in some man-to-man talk asked your father.
So light will be our wedding-band.

The other day I found an errant strand
Of your dark hair and held it, like a tether,
And though I never asked you for your hand,

We will be married, and
As this, hardly to be felt, twines round my finger,
So light will be our wedding-band.

So light that five years hence who could demand
Their freedom? From what, tied like this? Neither
Asked the other for their hand –

One London summer's morning it just happened.
The sun's rays wound gold heat about us there.
So light then was our wedding-band.

And you won't ask me to leave my rain-cursed land
Forever for your city with its saner weather.
I'll never ask you too. Give me your hand.
So light will be our wedding-band.

HÁJE

That's where we live. That's where the Metro loops
Back on itself and heads for town again.
That's where we step on escalating slopes
That draw us slowly up into the open
That's cleansed of trees; and massive concrete slabs,
Each studded with three hundred windows, icon
And estate, are simply everywhere.
A Marlboro billboard reminds me about nature.

That's where the city, driving southwards, ends
It's true (a smaller group of towerblocks noosed
By nothing, forest, wasteland where the highway bends
With freedom into open space, unloosed
At last and breaking from the city's bounds,
Nosedives for Wien), but nothing is released
Where nothing starts and stretches well-surveyed
To the horizon, toward which pylons stride and fade.

APARTMENT

You're drawn up to a tree's height in the air.
You leave the lift, unbolt the bolted door
And slam it shut behind you, home once more.
Relief. Unzip. Undress. Run the shower,

Unopened mail left waiting on the shelf.
Water scalds your body, steaming open
Your every pore, limbs slide around the soap in-
Side the tub. Step out and dry yourself.

Looking out the window, you see the forest,
Its black bar, the still-light sky and left
Of this another block, another lift,
Another hundred lives that felt the frost

In the fifteen minutes from the Metro home,
And lean back with a drink into the chair.
You watch one woman and then become aware
She's stopped her rhythmic strokes, put down her comb

And sees you. One instant and you have exchanged
It all. And nothing, when you twist the blinds
And turn back to your book that maybe binds
Huge things together, has everything arranged

From nations to the Derridean trace,
Voluted columns after columns of prose
That put things in perspective, balance praise
With scorn to hold the pantheon's roof in place.

It suddenly shivers like the trompe l'oeil
It maybe is beside the recent vision
Of a woman home from work, her earned seclusion,
So like you that you wonder if some play

Of light threw your reflection back into
Your drowsy eyes or you back into hers.
The moment of mirage and truth occurs
In the apartment buildings' interview,

A different kind of world from what you read,
A different kind of life from what you had
For years in that old house beneath the Hrad.
You find yourself inside this block of concrete

That's setting fast, like everybody else
Halfway to being bar-graphs, stacked in boxes
Across the south-town's *locus*
Un*amœnus* and dog-shit-covered green-belts.

And look at these, what's more, these ringing blocks
Laid down upon the whiteness of the page.
They try to draw you into their stiff cage.
(Whose wires are far too wide. Which no key locks.)

'Yes, and . . . ?' Well, life, as Joseph Cornell knew,
Is always an affair of different boxes.
Take these ones. Be my guest. What this place lacks is
Chaos. Impulse. Colour. Over to you.

BATHROOM

With cans of paint, some brushes and the radio
You disappeared today into the bathroom.
Incensed by its pure whiteness – enamelled rime
Of tiles and chalk-rough walls, their blinding ratio –

You came home yesterday with special paints
That hold their own on even those white surfaces'
Gloss and glare, and would metamorphose
Where we wash teeth, comb hair, keep stuff for pains

Into long panel after panel of blue
And yellow and green; a flower inside each one
Inside a room with no way in for sun –
A fight between the gridded immovables

And something that will always hate right angles
And smashes them to pieces when it wants,
But ends here in a startling détente
Of shapes and colours, just the few odd wrankles

Where brushstrokes overtake the tiling's bor-
Ders. All of which you kept a secret, locked
For hours in there. The only news that leaked
Was what the radio murmured under the door.

Swung open at long last as you mildly storm
Into the room to tell me it's on view,
Your hands still dripping yellows, greens and blues,
And touch me, colours flaring to my arm.

SIX HOUSEHOLD APPLIANCES

1   HOOVER

It picks up mainly pieces of us,
Small flakes of skin, odd hairs, an eyelash,
Then paperclips and grains of food
Gone hard where they fell three weeks past.

Every so often it's fit to burst
And there's this touching scene: the bag,
Split sometimes down the middle, is lifted
From the plastic vacuum chamber
And you can see it all conjoined
In wadded bliss at last: us there
With everything we sidelined, edged
Off tables, worktops, chairs and shelves
While forging our lives on ahead.

Dumped in the bin. The bag replaced.
And I'm off roaming round the flat
Again with this huge hungry wheeze,
This loud dog on a leash, resolved
To clean up, get our lives in order.

2   ICEBOX

How did a block of winter
End up inside this flat
Of creaking radiator,
Of nuclear-station heat,
This tropic where with languor
Palmettoes yawn and spread?

Ask rather how a towerblock
Of hottest summer stands
Oblivious to the bleak
Cold without. It astounds
To think about the deadlock
Temperatures and stunts

That winter pulls with snow
(The landscape overnight
Erased); how even so
We still survive inside
This cosy hell, how you
Will often walk bikini'd

While frost exfoliates
Across the window-pane.
Today, the radio states,
It could reach -13.
The icebox imitates
This chillingly alone.

It stores the sun for us –
For instance rock-hard blocks
Of vegetables, still fresh,
Whose complex photosynthetics
That once drew sunlight, freeze,
Put by as winter stocks.

Here too our spirits reside.
The vodka bottle frosted
While (contradiction stowed
In contradiction) the lustrous
Fluid moves inside.
It pours out, calm, unflustered,

Into the glass, itself
A glassy syrup. We've learnt
In deep December to slough
Off everything that's barren
With this small water. When quaffed
We feel its ice-cold burn.

Despite its tight corset
It stands full-bodied on the searing hob
   With one black arm akimbo. Of course it
Seethes the whole while long, since that's its job,

   But otherwise stands firm.
The little Java surging to its crown
   Does not erupt beyond its form
And make a Pompeii of the flat and town;

   I have to say I'm grateful.
As well as for the thimblefuls of tar
   That take god knows how many cratefuls
Of coffee bean to make, and months to mature.

   The grounds sit in their chamber
While underneath the water churns in turmoil
   Until the pressure and the temper-
Ature get to it and a gathering thermal

   Lifts it into flight.
It showers up through the perforated floor
   And infiltrates the cell outright.
The least and last ground is cleansed of all flavour.

   Then filtered by the moke
It bubbles up the home straight – huff and puff.
   See how the aperture gives a choke
And gushes forth the pure, the dark brown stuff.

   Which is all very well
Until you clean the tiny cauldrons out
   And prize apart the clam-tight shell
Inside of which the grounds adhese like grout:

   It's such a mess to wash.
The attitudes in which they came to grief –
   Sucked clean of essence by the whoosh
Of my need for refreshment and relief –

Those terror-stricken forms
Crumble like shale as the water takes its toll.
Across the sink they sweep enormous
Estuaries . . . then vanish down the plughole.

4   NUCLEAR REACTOR

Although it's rigged up in the middle
Of nowhere, it's our new cathedral,
Dead centre of a complex model
Of lines and cables, where polyhedral
Chains break down, the national griddle

That fries up isotopes for power.
The squabbles and the overreactions
That keep occurring hour after hour
With catalytic provocations
Inside the private chamber shower

Their energetic favours on
The land at large: for instance, cities,
Curved wide across the wide horizon,
Set midnight skies ablaze with these;
For instance, all the television

Unfolds with light in front of us
Is powered by these explosions; for instance,
Streetcars taking corners, office-
Buildings live with shares and options,
The hoover making handy refuse

Of our apartment clothed in dust –
Illuminations, metamorphoses
That arc through our all lives – induced,
You'll find if you sing back through fuses,
Wiring, against the electronic thrust,

If you go singing back and back
Through ten transformer stations, the grand
Systemic web that serves our lack,
All's brought to life by that hard grind
Of atoms underneath the stack.

Which leaves us at square one again.
The scope within that crucible!
How many times outstripping Röntgen's
These rays rebound and surge, unable
To break out, like tightly shackled dragons

Who if they find one crack will blow
The lot sky high; and then arise
And sweep through open cloudlands, billow,
Breathe, unfurl. And then erase
Everything their shadows touch below.

5   KETTLE

In Central Europe I placed a kettle on a hob
And waited in the kitchen. And from its watery depths,
From deep down at the element itself, the sound
Of North Atlantic surf came crashing storming out.

6   WASHING MACHINE

The dirty clothes
Have mounted up the whole week long
Inside the wicker basket:
Sudariums on which our loves and salts
Have left impressions – strong,
But getting rid of them won't blow a gasket.
Throw in the powder and start the waltz
Of clothes round clothes

Round clothes. Look in
And see the sudded galaxies
Of underwear and T-shirts,
Of jeans, of everything that makes us decent;
See how it all relaxes,
Like it doesn't give a damn and just reverts
To primal goulash, life unreasoned;
All this locked in

Until the drum
Comes whirling to a stop. Clean vapours
Fog the glass door-plate.
My hands reach deep inside and gather up
The mass of sodden fibres
That's like a soul, a dull amalgamate
Of our appearances, a pulp
Of styles so humdrum

You'd never think
That this is what we use to show
Our chic selves to the world.
The clothes must be dried out, ironed clean of crease
Before we'll let them go
About us – cuffs buttoned fast, belts tied, scarves furled –
And all our great civilities
Regained, we think.

The appliance dreams
Our habits through the nights and days:
Roused when drugged and blear,
Sent out into the world, brought back, a laugh,
Some film the machine replays,
Then spinned to sleep. That we assume we steer
Our lives is yet another of
Its programmed dreams.

SILENCE

November, and the sluggish orbits of a fly
Around the room are driving me insane.
It rests a second on the window pane
And my book flattens it against the sky.

That instant a truck outside starts grunting from its bonnet.
Give me a mountain range to swing down on it.
Give me a deadly viral strain that quells
The pounding of all next-door neighbours' blood cells.

SPYHOLE

My eyeball grooved into this hemisphere,
This stud of solid glass, I see the world
Beyond the door of our apartment swirled
Into strange shapes, as unreal as they're clear:

The white-walled corridor, fluorescent lights,
The other doors that wait there for an opening,
All comically bent round my eye, all sloping
Under duress in the lens's sights.

I lift my head away and suddenly
Things have the look of truth again: the chairs
Don't curl around my gaze, the table bears
Its load of fruit and papers steadily,

The walls keep floor from ceiling, perfectly flat
And upright. Unlike the curved grotesquerie
Kept safely outside under lock and key,
This is real. This is where we're at.

Or rather, I am, at the moment. You're
Beneath the city on the Metro home,
Making the transfers, straphanging to the hum
And racket of each subterranean contour.

I shadow you the last stretch, leaving the wagon,
Then up and past the upright ticket stocks
Into the night, between the dreaming towerblocks
To where you reach home and are real again.

INSOMNIA

We lie at night,
Blinds flush against
Streetlights burning
Five floors below.

We lie because
I sleep, you don't:
Statements of love,
We two are one,

Etc., these
Faded quickly
When I was dragged
By dark hands down

And out to where
A Buñuel film
Of my childhood
Is the feature.

I'm swimming through
Myself as through
A kind of dark
Marvellous honey.

Streetlights still burn
Your retinæ.
And you begin
To turn on me

Purely because
I sleep, you don't.
And toss, and burn,
And twist, and yearn

To be erased,
Your mind wiped clean
Of everything
It's ever known.

But not a chance.
Obstinately
And humming loud
As hell it goes

And goes and goes.
(He sleeps, I don't.
He sleeps, I don't.)
Then it doesn't

An hour or so.
And this is how
We lie at night,
Streetlights burning.

CHILDISHNESS

Dream-father, wind
Sweeps in across the forest, through the streets,
A ghost that howls its wound
Through every keyhole that it meets.

Dream-father, here
We have been cornered, in this apartment-block,
With its scream climbing higher,
Its plans to undo brick from brick,

Head over heels,
To smash us through the fields, across the highway,
Littered to the hills,
Our selves scaped out beneath the sky.

DREAM-FATHER: Wind,
It's only wind, which these shapes can withhold.
I know, for once I wound
Them tight about myself, my lovers, my world –

I've since untied,
And watched their continental-drift apart,
Salts of the earth that died,
But not before being loved, being part.

Up on the fifth floor
Of this benighted building, we lie in bed
And listen to rain scour
The windows angrily with beads.

We could doze off
And sleep through the storm's gathering furore –
Rain-punishments, explosive
Thunder, ray after cancer ray

Of nuclear wind –
And wake to find the city mobilised
In cars and buses, twinned
With somewhere on TV, policed

By foreign newsmen
Clambering for the best disaster shot.
And where would we be then,
Unhoused, unversed in that new plot,

Where everything
We know is wrong, no life left undenied,
No leg or stone left standing?
Why then, dream-father, then we'd need

The smallest hands
To heft our half-dead weight out of the old,
Work through the binding strands
And deliver us into the world.

Our childishness
Is such that it would take a child's small arms
To lift us up, judicious
Of our danger, and carry us from harm.

OR: we could fall
Asleep and wake to find the sunrise, a week
Of work ahead and all
Unmobilised, the storm a freak.

In which case we,
Dream-father, will do the same for it and slap
It wide awake. Rest easy.
Here's the morning. Now, *you* sleep.

HIGHLIGHTS

Last night the couple in the flat above us
Were in full flight: tirades and injured feelings
Swung back and forth for hours across the ceiling
Like bad jazz solos, long and repetitious.
Last week we caught crescendos from Sibelius.
And now tonight around eleven stealing
Through carpets and concrete slabs a wild, freewheeling
Moan of utter joy, which is their Anschluss.

But otherwise we'd never know they're there
And easily forget their sixth-floor sitcom.
We get on with our own lives – work and leisure,
Chores tending to our household appliances –
Which seem the same as theirs (the noise, the rhythm)
Apart from what goes on between, in silence.

NEW APARTMENT:
TERENURE, 1968

Stacked and scattered here and there
About the main room of the flat
The boxes, chairs and bulging suitcases
Have skidded to a sudden standstill.
My parents start arranging things.
They bring the table to the kitchen,
Considering its shape and size
Against the kitchen's for a minute,
Then place one edge against the wall.
They unstrangle lamps of their flexes.
They try to imagine their future life
With the new couch there, or there,
As though the choice that they make now
Will set them on one course for years.

The TV is a square of solid shadow
Securely housed in imitation teak.

Switched on. A phosphorescence starts to speak.
They watch the country turning through a talk-show.

The country stretches to the rocks
And sand and cliffs and promenades
Which mark the island's end; the fields
And hills and that one rainy street
Through which the border runs; standing
Idly by itself in mohair,
With patriotic decency.
The floor space of their new apartment
Makes up one tiny tract of this.

Free of their parents' furniture and prints
They love to plan and switch and rearrange.

Things brim with possibility, with change.
Themselves in three months to become new parents.

For six or seven days they labour
To make the cosmos I'll inhabit.
I orbit in my mother's stomach
Oblivious to the fact that soon
I will be made to move as well.

THE MOVING HOUSE

for Shane and David

I'm thirteen. We're in a car
That westers with a caravan in tow.
Nobody's speaking in my nuclear
Family just now entering Mayo.
Transported miles from home, round lakes,
Up into clouds by virtue
Of the winding mountain-route the trunk road takes,
Past fields and valleys, the odd fine view
For which we stop, religiously
Alight, are told to 'take that in'
(Both the parents sigh),
And then are stuffed into the car again,
The road resumed, the hedgerows and the fields
Along the roadside blurring by,
Us slumping back into the seats,
We're on our holiday.

★

No, it began, in fairness,
Once the caravan was parked and jacked down fast,
When we would start right off to furnish
It with all the stuff devised
To make our home from home, well, civil.
Everything from the mat,
The teacups, clothesline, **Swingball**™, shovel,
To, dazed by this strange move, our mutt.
We thought it was hilarious,
His nervous scampering everywhere
To mark the place with piss,
The way he checked it and rechecked it, unclear
As to how the house could put on wheels and move
Into a field (hmm, have a scratch)
By sea and mountains. Of course, he'd have
To keep a careful watch.

★